MW01244717

WAITING FOR PRINCE

CHARMING IN THE REAL WORLD

SALLY SMALE

Enjoy the "ride"!

Sally
Smale

Copyright @ 2016 by Sally Smale
All rights reserved.
No part of this publication may be reproduced, stored in a
retrieval system, or transmitted in any form or by any
means – electronic, mechanical, photocopy, recording, or
any other form without the prior permission of the author
and publisher.

ISBN-13: 978-1536986150

Scripture references are as noted:
NLT –   New Living Translation
AMP – Amplified Bible
NIV –   New International Version
NKJV - New King James Version
ESV –   English Standard Version
MSG – The Message

Cover design by Crystal Magallanes

Author photo by Jessica Rice

Establishing Word Ministries
www.establishingword.com

To my husband, children, and family – you have loved me and always encouraged me to do and be all that God dreamed for me. Without your constant support, this project would not have been possible.

Most of all, I dedicate this book to my Prince Charming, my True Love, Jesus Christ. Every day You pour out Your extravagant love upon me. Not only have You given me a new life, but You have taught me the meaning of love. I am Yours forever!

CONTENTS

SECTION I
Fairytale vs. Reality

1. Growing Up in Make-believe…………...Pg 1
2. All Grown Up in the Real World……...Pg 7

SECTION II
The Great Quest

3. Looking For Love in All the Wrong Places………………………………..Pg 15
4. Unlikely Places………………………Pg 19
5. The Prince has Come……………….Pg 23

SECTION III
Invited to the Ball

6. Meeting Someone New…………….........Pg 29
7. The Proposal …………………….….......Pg 35

SECTION IV
Wedding Preparations

8. Attending to Details…………………Pg 41
9. The Wedding Dress and Trousseau….Pg 45
10. The Carriage Ride…………………....Pg 51
11. Staying Busy While We Wait………......Pg 59
12. Your Invitation Has Arrived ………...Pg 65
    About the Author………………….....Pg 69

SECTION I

FAIRYTALE VS. REALITY

CHAPTER 1

GROWING UP IN MAKE-BELIEVE

L et's face it, no matter how hard you and I try, we each bring our imperfect past into our today. As the history of disappointments and rejection are replayed over and over in our mind, we become convinced that no one will ever truly love and accept us. But what if I told you that your Prince is indeed out there and his love for you will be perfect and unconditional?

A child's imagination is often stimulated by action and adventure stories. These tales usually involve a battle between good and evil. Heroes and heroines fight with unearthly strength and power. Within the scope of a child's knowledge, such things seem far beyond their future ability to grasp or attain. Physically, these characters are specimens of perfection in a young minds' eyes and have one very important common denominator. Superheroes and heroines always win! The victories they obtain are always followed by a declaration of "and they lived happily ever after".

No matter how good our childhood may be, it will never measure up to the fantasy of the fairytale. If you have had children or been around them, you probably are aware of their tendency to dramatize and exaggerate incidents that are not only harmless, but necessary to their training and development. We have all seen a child dissolve into tears or act out in anger at a stern look, a raised voice, or (beyond comprehension!) the word "no". It's easy, then, to see that any disappointment or alteration of their perception of the ideal might be exaggerated as a misery from which they need rescued. Even in the most generous and loving families, these stories can provide a place of fictional perfection that is impossible to duplicate in real life.

The truth is, no matter how hard we try we all bring our own histories of imperfect pasts into our todays. We arrive with broken and tattered luggage, barely held together with a string of coping mechanisms we've learned to keep us functioning comfortably in uncomfortable situations. Our wedding day promises the hope of a clean slate- a place where we can create the ideal life and love story we dreamed of our whole lives. Then we begin to "unpack" our bags. What comes out inevitably affects our relationship and our parenting. We believe that what our parents said and did to us will keep us from repeating the same behavior with our children. The truth is that children really do learn what they live. Consequently, we see patterns of abuse, neglect, abandonment, and all kinds of "imperfections" carried across generations.

I remember, as a child who lived in the reality of a broken and abusive home, hours of escape into worlds where a prince charming would swoop in on a beautiful white stallion, rescue the fair maiden in distress (me), and carry her away from worry, fear, trouble, heartache, and pain to live that imagined life of pure bliss. Even today, memories of sitting on an open vent blowing warm air while wrapped in a blanket with my favorite books can spark feelings of comfort and joy. Perhaps that is the reason that I can picture the countless number of children who devour and cling to these stories as a way to survive each day in the midst of unspeakable horrors of pain and torment. They are temporarily sustained by the possibilities of "true happiness". Even as children, we have a longing to search for the better life that we somehow know exists outside of our circumstances.

We rejoice with our kids over the happy endings as we read the stories to them. We laugh at the clumsy, slow-witted "bad guys" and cheer when the underdog is promoted to a place of acceptance and recognition as we watch the television programs and the movies as a family. It is our desire as parents to encourage and reinforce a positive image of life that will help them to reach for the best- the best education, the best job, the best friends, the best spouses, and the best families. We pray that we have equipped them and given them a solid foundation on which they can build a happy life. When it is time for them to venture out on their own, we not-so-confidently close our eyes and let them go. Will they be able to overcome the evil in this world and find their "happily ever after"? After all, things look a lot different out there than when we were kids.

"When I was a child, I spoke and thought and reasoned as a child. But when I grew up, I put away childish things."
1 Corinthians 13:11 (NLT)

CHAPTER 2

ALL GROWN UP IN THE REAL WORLD

Do you remember the old TV shows like "The Donna Reed Show" or "Father Knows Best"? Okay, so maybe you saw an old rerun of these black and white shows as you were flipping through the stations. Regardless, you may have noticed that they were created in a time when the media esteemed and portrayed a very different point of view of the family and our society than the ones being proliferated by our modern media and culture. In the past, it was every little girl's dream to grow up to be a wife who stayed at home to cook, clean, and take care of the children. It was an honor to serve their families in this way. Granted, these programs portrayed an ideal of performing all of these duties dressed in their Sunday best, wearing high-heeled shoes and pearls, while sporting a huge smile no matter what situation was unfolding. Believe me when I tell you that in all of the years of my experience as a wife, mother, and grandmother, I have never (not even one time!) met a woman who could live up to that ideal! I could tell you many a tale about days raising three boys that ended with my poor husband coming home to a scene quite different than these. Days when there wasn't even a break to take a shower, let alone remove the sweatpants and comb the disheveled hair that I had been trying to keep from pulling out while being referee to countless arguments and wrestling matches. Makeup and dresses were not even in my man's wildest dreams! He merely aspired to pull me down off of the ceiling long enough to calm me down, wipe my tears, and play with the kids long enough for me to make dinner! And that was okay by me.

In the 1960's and 70's, the Women's Liberation Movement (later referred to as the Feminist Movement) emerged as women began to fight for equality with men and be liberated from this picture of the woman's role. Shouts of "I am woman, hear me roar!" were heard above the crackling of bonfires lit for the sole purpose of burning bras that represented the bondage of the modern woman. Let me say that I believe that women have the ability to excel in all areas of education, the work force, as well as in the home (albeit preferably in jeans). I know that hindsight is 20/20, but the fact that I grew up during those times has given me the ability to look retrospectively over the years that have followed. Allow me to state some of my observations.

There is an attitude of "independent strength" that has grown from this movement that seems to isolate women (especially from men) and guards against any thought of needing or giving assistance. Young women have been taught that they can "have it all"- multiple-degreed educations, high-paying and powerful jobs, happy marriages or many self-satisfying partners, perfect children (with or without the help of a husband or even a man), and the gorgeous mansion in the perfect location. Now, if we examine that list, we can easily see that there have been impossible ideals set up for our girls to reach. Each one of those goals alone would take tireless

9

effort and attention without being extended to include any of the others. Ladies, as strong and wonderfully talented as we are, we are still only one person. And there are still only 24 hours in every day. As a result of this ongoing "superwoman" mentality, unprecedented pressures have been put on women. When things don't go as they have been diligently planned, or when they collapse in a pile of dirty laundry from sheer exhaustion, they wonder what went wrong and where they have failed.

Add to this mountain of expectations a very different state of our nation's economy, and it ushers in a shift in cultural views. Now, a high percentage of women MUST work- whether they want to or not. It is necessary for there to be two incomes in order to make ends meet. On top of the stresses previously discussed, society has heaped the addition of a generous helping of guilt! The working mom feels guilty because she must leave her home and her children in order to bring in extra income. The stay-at-home mom feels guilty because she is not "pulling her weight" and bringing in extra income. Manufacturers took advantage of the state of chaos in the hearts of women by advertising a bubble bath that could "take us away" from all of the madness. Who wouldn't want to buy some of that? With the mounting stresses and pressures of life today in this world, is it really so hard to explain the rise in the divorce rate and what we have become to believe is normal to be a part of a "dysfunctional" family? Everyone is so tightly wound in a bundle of raw nerves that explosive verbal and emotional abuse can be triggered with little provocation. Physical and sexual abuse can arise in the midst of perceived power struggles and the need for money and control. No amount of soaking in tubs of bubble bath will provide more than a temporary escape- and that's if the kids aren't beating on the door (or each other) to redirect your attention to their "emergencies".

Is it any wonder that we try to find strength and hope from the possibility of our childhood fairytales coming true for us? Let's be honest with ourselves! Haven't we all at one time or another dreamed of that escape out of life's struggles into a perfect world? Your grown-up head tells you that it is all imagined and impossible, but your heart argues that there might

11

be a place where make-believe and truth collide. Although you move through life trying to manage the harsh reality of your days as they unfold, there is a constant longing to fill the gnawing emptiness that screams, "Surely, there has to be more than this!"

"But understand this, that in the last days there will come (set in) perilous times of great stress and trouble – hard to deal with and hard to bear."   2 Timothy 3:1 (AMP)

SECTION II

THE GREAT QUEST

CHAPTER 3

LOOKING FOR LOVE IN ALL THE WRONG PLACES

The perceived cause of the "empty abyss" will be different for everyone. But you can be certain, we all have it. For me, finding out that my conception had been the product of an extramarital affair and, consequently, being raised in a home where love was shown in angry and conditional terms left me with a feeling of no worth or value. I was a mistake. There was no planned purpose or reason for my life. After years of trying to earn my "Daddy's" love and always coming up short, I determined in my adolescent heart that there must be someone, somewhere who would love me for who I was and just because I exist. I began a journey, guided by the driving force of rejection, which I was sure would eventually lead to finding my prince charming.

As previously mentioned, our culture bombards our young people with promises of great worth and value in life if they receive the best education, are able to affix multiple letters after their signatures, and ascend to the top of their chosen profession. What we're not told is that there are no guarantees no matter how hard you try. I was good in school. I was able to excel academically with only the occasional B+ showing up on my report card. Every parent's dream, right? But it was never quite good enough. Those less-than-perfect grades brought me just to the edge of acceptance, but kept me yearning on the outskirts of unconditional love and acceptance.

The 1960's exploded with a revolution of drugs and "free" sex and, with it, a generation of youth who experimented with a "new" way to feel that love and acceptance. We have all known, seen, or have been a casualty of the heartache of drug abuse and addiction. The escape from reality is temporary, and the reality of life's pain becomes drastically increased when the "high" wears off. Mere moments of experiencing that free-fall from being in control into the overwhelming sense of peace and well-being have led many to lose careers, marriages, families, and their very lives.

I was on a mission to take control of my own life. Because of this, I resisted being drawn into the drug culture. I was, nonetheless, intoxicated by the realization that I could cause those of the opposite sex to enter my world with just a seductive look or an "innocent" game of flirting, a discovery that was just as addicting as the substances I had vowed to avoid. I continued my pursuit all the while hoping that maybe if even one got close enough to get to know the real me, they might love me! The old, familiar charge of "If you really loved me, you would show me!" became the dreaded mantra of relationship after relationship. I was so wounded and desperate in my search for love that I was willing to give anything to find it. Even the most valuable thing I owned. Me. Every time they tired of me, a part of me was ripped away with them as they walked out of my life. Each one only confirmed what I believed to be true. I was not worthy to be loved.

Eventually, along came a guy who didn't tell me that the only thing I was good for was sex. He was different.   He treated me like I had value that surpassed my abilities to bring him physical pleasure. He was kind and cared about the things that were important to me.   For the first time in my life here was a man that promised to provide all I wanted in a husband and the children that would be the center of my world.   All of that plus giving me an unending supply of the love I needed.   At last, my prince charming had come to take me away to Happily Ever After!

He could never take me there.   Nobody is capable of being everything to us. Another part of the fairytale tells us that our prince charming is our "soul mate" and will "complete" us.   I was too broken for him to fix me. After years of expecting him to fill my empty void and trying what the world offered as "help" for troubled marriages, I was done. The attorney had been called.   Once again, I was going to take control of my life and continue on in the illusive quest for real, true love.

"Why do you look for the living among [those who are] dead? Luke 24:5 (AMP)

CHAPTER 4

UNLIKELY PLACES

Perhaps you came from a wonderful family that displayed love. Maybe you have attained your educational, financial, and career goals. You might also have a good marriage and happy home. I sincerely applaud you and rejoice with you! Yet, I know there is still a part of you that wants more. And that doesn't make you ungrateful or a bad person. It makes you human. We all have a longing to fill an emptiness that continues to escape satisfaction no matter how much we achieve in life. It becomes our motivating force and life's purpose even though we may deny its very existence. It compels us to search in all the wrong places. We pursue status, money, power, and relationships.

I found myself pregnant with my second child while in the middle of my life's turmoil. Even though

I had given up on my marriage, I still clung to the hope that I could somehow give to my children and receive from them the love I had never known. What I never considered was the fact that I had never experienced that kind of love. In fact, I had never even seen it modeled as an example I might be able to manufacture. No matter, I thought if I could be the best mother to them, the feeling of emptiness in my life would subside. I became absorbed with finding ways to make childbirth and parenting more natural and healthy.

I started attending monthly meetings with women who were more experienced and personally practiced that lifestyle. I enjoyed their company so much that I began to hang around after the official meeting ended. I was intrigued by the friendship of these women who also had seemingly insurmountable problems in their own lives, yet they seemed to have an underlying peace and joy that escaped me. They never excluded me because of my differing opinions or made me feel like an outsider because they had known each other for many years.

After months of getting well acquainted, we began to openly share our struggles. I cried as I told them about my unfulfilled quest for love and acceptance. Instead of the scorn and rejection I was expecting, arms were gently wrapped around me and a love I had never experienced before was lavished upon me. It was a kind of love that was totally unfamiliar to me. They expected nothing in return. They looked at me through eyes of understanding and compassion instead of criticism and judgement.

We all want an instant fix. But the walls I had erected around my hardened heart were slow to dismantle. After many hours of willing sacrifice and wisdom sprinkled with gentleness, the patience of these amazing women was rewarded as my heart was softened and opened up to receive the truth they were trying to convey. God made us all with that longing that I had been trying to fill with everything else but Him. I wasn't the only one who felt this way! In fact, that longing is part of the plan to lead us into His loving arms. They told me that I wasn't a big mistake. I was planned even before I was born with a specific purpose in this world! I was loved. The arguments in my head (and those rushing out of my mouth) were fueled by lies and words that I had been told my whole life. Could this possibly be true? Was there really One who could heal my broken heart and take away the emptiness of my unfulfilled quest? My Prince Charming?

"He has made everything beautiful in its time; He also has planted eternity in men's hearts and minds [a divinely implanted sense of purpose working through the ages which nothing under the sun but God alone can satisfy]... Ecclesiastes 3:11 (AMP)

CHAPTER 5

THE PRINCE HAS COME

There is only one Prince with the ability to love perfectly and unconditionally. He knows us best, and loves us most. He provides a place of absolute safety- a shelter and refuge from our daily battles. He is rich and generous. He can unveil our life's purpose and give direction as our constant companion on the path to fulfilling it. His name is Jesus Christ. He alone is able to fill the emptiness in our lives with the greatest love we will ever know.

The Bible tells us in 1 John 19 that we can only really love because He loved us first. He knew us and called us by name before the very foundations of the earth and had a plan for our lives in mind when we were formed in our mother's womb. There's no need to waste time worrying over whether or not He will uncover the dirty little secrets you have hidden from your past. He already knows everything about you! How refreshing to have a relationship where everything is out on the table. You have freedom to speak what is on your heart and in your mind because, well, He already knows it's there and wants to make it all okay. You are the "apple of His eye" and His heart's delight. His thoughts are always about you to bring good and not harm into your life. In fact, there's even a tattoo of your name on His hand!

Sound too good to be true? We learn early on in our experiences that when it sounds too good to be true, it usually is. We become suspicious and cynical about selfless behavior or unsolicited kindness. We've all been that one "waiting for the other shoe to drop". The walls we build around our hearts for protection are the very things that keep us from finding the answers for which we've spent our lives searching.

The wall around my heart was tall and wide. When my newfound friends would talk to me about Jesus, I would agonize over every man that had ever entered my life- from father (or fathers in my case), right up to the husband who had fallen extremely short of meeting my expectations. Every single one of them had hurt me and left me with deep scars of disappointment and mistrust, not to mention the overwhelming insecurities that followed me into every situation I encountered. I had set out on the road to independence! I didn't need anyone else in my life-especially another MAN! I am not exaggerating when I tell you I was in so much turmoil that it began to affect me physically. The stomachaches and trips to the bathroom increased as I fought with the possibility that there really was a prince who will, indeed, come on a white horse and take us with Him to live our "happily ever after". My heart longed to believe, but my mind was tormented by memories of the past and the realities of my present situation. I had tried counseling and most everything else our world has to offer to ease my pain and heal my wounds. Nothing worked. For eight solid months, those surprisingly persistent women lovingly and patiently continued to lead me forward, all the while knowing that I had given up hope of ever finding lasting fulfillment in any relationship. They answered my multitudes of questions which would always leave me seeking for truth in the book they knew so well. But the Bible was not just any book to them. It seemed to contain some kind of magical power that enabled them to live in a way that seemed contrary to their circumstances. I didn't understand it, but a trickle of hope sprung up from way down deep inside of me. And then the invitation came.

"His name shall be called Wonderful Counselor, Mighty God, Everlasting Father, and Prince of Peace." Isaiah 9:6b (NIV)

SECTION III

INVITED TO THE BALL

CHAPTER 6

MEETING SOMEONE NEW

I know the President of the United States of America. Well, I know all about him. I know things he has said because of the ability to record his speeches. I even know about his family and his hobbies. But is it true for me to claim to know the man? Will he accept my calls and tell me the secret things hidden in his heart? I think not! His bride, however, has his ear at all times and shares an intimate relationship with him. Their connection likely began after they met face to face and she accepted his invitation to go on a date.

That's the same way we enter into a relationship with Jesus. You may have heard about Him your whole life. Maybe you even visit His house once in a while where you hear stories that sound good, but never affect your life in any way. One day, because of longing and searching for that great love, we come face to face with Him. Just like Prince Charming, He invites us to the ball. He extends His hand, and we have the choice to accept or reject His invitation.

By this time, I had done a great deal of research and thought I knew everything I needed to know about Jesus. My head was full of ideas and thoughts concerning the possibilities, but I kept myself just beyond reach. Instead, I watched from a distance as my friends were enjoying everything I desired. It became obvious that the next step was up to me. The introduction had been made, but if I was going to experience the intimate and unconditional love that Jesus promised to give me, I would have to take the huge risk of opening my well-guarded heart to yet another relationship and claim Him as my own.

New relationships are hard. There's always that awkward time when you're first getting acquainted. You know, that time when you want them to be honest and real, but you are still dancing around the truth of who you really are. This was especially true for me because of the string of past rejections that followed me into every new encounter. I had trained myself to enter a room, check out who was there, and determine what mask or persona I would become to be liked and accepted. I became so good at it, that I didn't even have to give it much thought anymore. And I was highly successful! People seemed to enjoy being around me and I learned how to make them laugh, even when I was crying on the inside. Smokey Robinson's song, "Tears of a Clown", became the theme song of my life. If everyone saw that I was the life of the party, then nobody would guess just how broken and hurting I really was.

It was Mother's Day, significant because it had become my favorite holiday. It honored the one thing in my life that gave it meaning and purpose. That day, I made the decision to overcome my logic and hesitations. I accepted the invitation and stepped into a relationship with Jesus. Just like with any new relationship, I had the giddy feeling of hope and promise. But this time, it was different. I went from merely hoping, to a deep-settled assurance and knowledge that somehow my life was about to be turned upside down. Peace washed over me. Though none of my circumstances had changed, I experienced a joy that I couldn't explain. Then there was the love.

I had told Him everything I had ever done and how miserable and sorry I was for the mess I had made of everything. He didn't reject me, condemn me, or make me feel more shame. Instead, He lavished this love on me that began the process of change.

Now, I had tried to change myself so many times before in so many ways. Living in our home was a toddler who inevitably waited until his grandparents were visiting to accurately mimic the colorful language he had heard coming from his mama's mouth. Even I knew it was time to clean it up! Old habits never want to die. As hard as I tried, I failed miserably. One of the first things that happened to prove to me this was not going to be just any new relationship was that I stopped cussing. I mean completely stopped! This may not be a big deal to you, but it was huge for me. I had tried everything, including the ever-popular "Swear Jar". You know, the one where you run out of coins because you stubbed your toe or stepped on a Lego? Maybe Jesus was just showing off to lure me in deeper, but this totally got my attention! My husband, who had not yet made His acquaintance, took notice with weird side glances as the deluge of profanity disappeared. More importantly, there were changes happening on the inside that were beginning to show on the outside. Defensiveness, anger, unforgiveness, and resentment were beginning to be whittled away. Instead of lashing out at my husband, I became quiet. (Well, quiet for me!) My focus was no longer on trying to change everyone else. All I wanted was to pursue the new relationship I had discovered. This Jesus had made Himself known clearly in my life and I now had a mad crush on Him and was falling head over heels in love.

"Ask, and it will be given to you; seek, and you will find; knock, and it will be opened to you." Matthew 7:7 (NKJV)

CHAPTER 7

THE PROPOSAL

L ike anyone in the throes of an exciting new romance, I wanted to spend every minute with my love. I had an insatiable desire to get to know Jesus up close and personally. I devoured the Bible every spare moment. I remember reading while I was doing laundry, cooking, and the kids were playing. The amazing thing was that I started to hear Him talk to me from the pages. I waited patiently for nap time so I could talk to Him. Late into the night, I would talk to Him about every imaginable topic. I found that I could easily uncover what was really on my heart with no fear.

I love getting gifts. Who doesn't, right? Let's be honest. We enter into a relationship looking for what we can get out of it. What will I get for my time invested? When the flowers and chocolates start to arrive and all of the attention is on us, we feel valued and adored. Jesus wins, hands down, in the showering with gifts department. It seemed like every question and request was answered- sometimes so quickly it took my breath away. His love was shown to me in the common, little things of life that proved He was interested in the details of my life. I have come to call those times "kisses from God". Even now, no matter how tough my day might be, these special kisses can stop me in my tracks and make me take notice. I'm once again reminded that I am loved.

Because I had never known true love before, this relationship was extremely one-sided. I must admit that I was extremely happy and quite satisfied with the way things were going. I had finally found someone whose only interest was me. I was special and, apparently, the center of the universe. During this courtship, I became keenly aware that His thoughts were constantly focused on me and that I was His delight.

Just when I thought everything was going so well, I heard Him pop "the" question, "Will you marry Me?". Before you think I've taken leave of my senses, I understand that I already had a husband, and

I assure you I didn't hear an audible voice. It was simply a thought that resonated deep within my heart and one I was unable to ignore. I was intrigued enough to seriously examine this relationship. I had been content to date Jesus. Oh, I was willing to spend a lot of time with Him (when it was convenient to fit into my busy schedule), and certainly receive all that was given to me because, after all I had been through, it was about time and I deserved it.

Immediately, memories of rejection and fears of being alone seemed to suffocate me. Was I really ready to surrender everything? The past only confirmed that this, too, would end in rejection and abandonment. Everyone's on their best behavior when they are dating. Marriage means not only sharing everything, but being committed to grow and even sacrifice for the other person. It involves trust. That had become a nasty word in my vocabulary that I had greatly avoided and nearly forgotten. I had vowed that I would never trust anyone again with my whole heart. Why should this time be any different?

As the days progressed, I was being wooed. I know that's an old fashioned word, but it's the only one I can think of to describe what was going on inside of me. Jesus pursued me in such a way that I found myself wanting nothing more than Him. There were times that His presence was so real to me, I could feel His arms wrapped around me. I was positive that if I opened my eyes, He would be sitting right there beside me. It was during those sweet times together that I started feeling secure in His love, and my fears began to slowly melt away. He had given me a new life, washed me clean from all of the dirt of my past, and loved me unconditionally. He gave everything to me without hesitation or expectation. Now it was time that I did the same. This was no longer going to be a superficial, lopsided relationship. He had brought me from the selfishness of "What can I get?" to a deeper, more mature love that finally was able to ask, "What can I do for You?", and really mean it. He had already made His desire known to my heart. We were betrothed!

"Arise, my love, my beautiful one, and come away, for behold, the winter is past, the rain is over and gone." Song of Solomon 2:10-11 (ESV)

SECTION IV

WEDDING PREPARATIONS

CHAPTER 8

ATTENDING TO DETAILS

Fairytales always include a big, glorious wedding. It's the wedding of every little girl's dream. With all of the details that need to be carefully planned and executed with perfection, it can take a very long time to prepare. Actually, there are those of us who have been planning this big event since we were teenagers or even younger. Some were organized enough to have scrapbooks with pictures of what we wanted for our big day cut out of every magazine we got our hands on. The images of the perfect flowers, centerpieces, table settings, color schemes, and maybe even a theme for the occasion were carefully placed on the pages. There were hairstyles that looked good with our veil choices or tiaras (for every proper princess), and even flowers that were meticulously placed on a headpiece or in the hair to accent the beauty of the bride. Entire sections of the book were filled with all the dresses. Who knew there were so many different ones to choose from? And then there were the shoes and jewelry, not to mention the gifts for the bridesmaids and groomsmen. We wanted everything to be just the way we had always dreamed- perfect in every way!

The truth is, many couples get overwhelmed with all of the planning and looming expense and decide to surprise everyone by secretly eloping. No matter what kind of wedding is taking place, the bride always sets the date. Well, at least, the bride and groom hash it out until an acceptable date for both of them can be chosen. Imagine my shock when I found out that I would have no say in when my upcoming wedding to my betrothed was to take place! The Bible clearly states that no one knows the day and hour when Jesus will come to receive His bride and take her to be with Him for all eternity. It seems that all of us who have committed ourselves to Jesus are the ones who are going to be surprised! There will be no time for any unfinished business. When He comes, we have to be ready to go. Well, how in this world can we make that happen? Just like any wedding, it will take effort. And time- lots of time! The more time we invest in getting ready, the better we will be prepared and ready for the main event.

There is a story in the Bible (Matthew 25:1-13) about a bunch of women who were waiting for their groom as well. Like me, they didn't know when to expect him. This was written so long ago that electricity hadn't yet been invented. They used oil lamps to light their houses and to see where they were going in the dark. Like many of us, half of them became impatient. I imagine they were even beginning to doubt whether or not he was going to come for them at all. Instead of working diligently to have everything in order for his arrival, they decided to take a nap. As the story unfolds, their lamps ran out of oil. The unprepared girls tried to get some from the girls that were diligently preparing, but they needed every bit of oil they had to give light for what they were doing to get ready for the groom's return. Sadly, while those who had chosen to nap were searching out the local all-night market for a fill-up, their man had come and they missed him! To add to their dismay, they had to live with the knowledge that all the other brides were ready and were living their happily-ever-after.

I get impatient, too. I long for the day when I will finally see Jesus face to face and He will take me away to sit with Him and eat the best food I've ever had at a wedding. One of the greatest things about this meal is that I don't have to make any of the arrangements for it! The menu, as well as the table settings, are being prepared now and I can simply sit back and enjoy the celebration with the one true love of my life. He's in charge of getting it all ready with the things I like best and some I haven't yet discovered. As I have mentioned earlier, I love gifts. I cannot wait to see what amazing presents are waiting for me to arrive and unwrap! But, alas, I'm determined to make myself busy while I wait. I want to look my very best when I arrive and there's still so much to do.

"But in your hearts revere Christ as Lord. Always be prepared..." 1 Peter 3:15 (NIV)

CHAPTER 9

THE WEDDING DRESS AND TROUSSEAU

I t's a well-known fact that most women love clothes. We carefully look through fashion magazines and watch TV programs and ads to keep up with the latest styles. Remember all of the pictures in our scrapbooks? We stand in our closets trying on outfit after outfit to come up with the right combination for that special meeting or occasion. If we don't find it there, we have the perfect excuse for a shopping trip. We venture into the fitting room with our arms full of promising possibilities. Inevitably, we will wind up in front of the mirror. I will concede that there are a few of you out there that may have a figure like one of the mannequins in the department stores. I do not. I never have. Mirrors only remind me of how very far I am from what I am apparently supposed to look like.

When it comes to our wedding dress and the clothes we will take into our future, we think we have to do whatever is necessary to miraculously transform ourselves into this image. Weeks of dieting and starvation, coupled with excessive exercise leave us teetering on the brink of collapsing into an unhealthy heap of weakness and frailty. We convince ourselves that it will be worth it in the end. The problem is, it's never quite enough. Somehow, with a conspicuously missing glam squad of stylists, makeup artists, and airbrushes, the everyday woman can never reach those ideals. Why do we unendingly look to the media and our cultural standards to decide what will make us a beautiful bride? No matter what the mirror tells us, we still struggle with our outward appearance. The ironic part about it is that even those skinny, unblemished girls we've been comparing ourselves to don't like what they see either!

As I continued my preparations, I discovered that the Bible is also a mirror. The more I read, the more I saw my flaws and imperfections. Sadly, I discovered a great deal more than all of the mirrors in my life to this point had exposed. These were those things that had attached themselves to me at a very young age and I had carried them all through my life without even knowing they were there. There was rejection, unforgiveness, bitterness, resentment, and anger to name a few. Then there were the hidden things. You know, those things we don't let people know about. I had built walls of protection around my broken heart. Nobody was going to get close to the fears and wounds that left me insecure and vulnerable. I had promised myself that I would never allow anyone into those secret rooms hidden beneath a façade of strength and confidence. The past had proven to me that any weaknesses I showed would be immediately judged and I would be found unworthy.

I was getting closer to Jesus every day until the unimaginable happened. He captured my heart! I knew things were changing when I began to actually desire that He know the real me- not the illusion I had been presenting to the world. His love was so pure, so kind and gentle, that He lured me to trust Him. Hesitantly, I began to unwrap what was in my heart as I pleaded for a way out. Tears flowed (and still do to this day) as I felt Him cleanse me and heal me. I had finally found it- true, unconditional love! Though He didn't necessarily like the things I was showing Him, there was never a sense of judgment or rejection. Instead, He looked at me and saw what He knew I was destined to become. There was an understanding that, if I gave permission and continued to trust, He would never leave me and would take me by the hand and walk with me every step of the way. How overjoyed I was to discover that He didn't look at me the way others had looked. When I thought I had to look to the world and the standards of our society when deciding on my wedding dress, I found out that Jesus wanted to clothe me according to His design!

While the rest of the world is all caught up in what we look like on the outside, this Prince Charming is most concerned about what we look like on the inside. The Bible tells of His bride being presented to Him in garments of white. That sounds like a wedding dress to me! But weaved into the very fabric of the gown is what He considers beautiful. Something that is more amazing than any lace or satin. The secret fiber is righteousness. Don't worry.

I flipped out, too, when I read that word! After everything I had been through and everything I had tried to do to change in order to make myself better, how could I possibly be expected to live anything that came close to righteousness? I was already clearly aware that I was not perfect and didn't need reminded of it. However, just as clear to me was the knowledge that Jesus *is* perfect. The only reminding that He did was to tell me yet again that He wanted to do this in me and for me if I would trust and allow Him access. And so began the tedious task of clothing me.

Unfortunately, some brides believe that in order to look beautiful and be accepted they have to appeal to the desires of men. That usually means the less fabric the better. Very early on, I realized that the creating of the garments I was going to wear would not only include a lot of material, but would take a very long time to make. Actually, it takes a lifetime. Every time we choose forgiveness over offense, more is added. When we make the decision to be kind instead of self-serving, the process continues. The parts woven with the love we show when we live our life as a reflection of the love we have found in our relationship with Jesus is the most beautiful and dazzling of all. It's unfathomable. It's simply divine! I've come to the conclusion that I want the biggest, fullest wedding gown with the longest train you've ever seen.

"So, chosen by God for this new life of love, dress in the wardrobe God picked out for you: compassion, kindness, humility, quiet strength, discipline. Be even-tempered, content with second place, quick to forgive an offense. Forgive as quickly and completely as the Master forgave you. And regardless of what else you put on, wear love. It's your basic, all-purpose garment. Never be without it." Colossians 3:12-14 (MSG)

CHAPTER 10

THE CARRIAGE RIDE

I am a hopeless romantic and love stories about how the women from the pages of history used to take long, extended periods of time for beauty treatments before seeing their lovers. Cleopatra bathed in milk with honey, used sea salt body scrub way before it became popular, and applied the best in local Egyptian cosmetics to get ready for a date with Marc Antony. One of the longest beauty treatments in history has to be that of Queen Esther in the Bible. Before her wedding night, she spent 12 whole months of soaking and smearing. No kidding! The first six months were with oil, and the last six months were with special perfumes and ointments. Like any other girl, I'm all in for a good pampering before the Big Day, but who's got time for *that*? We take a shower or bath, shave the usual places, and hopefully have remembered to fit in a mani/pedi. Finally, we throw everything in the car and pray that we haven't forgotten anything and that the ones in charge of hair and makeup don't get lost and show up late to the designated meeting place. Talk about stress that can be a real mood killer!

Because of my love for a good story that's infused with romance, my favorite book in the Bible is the Song of Solomon. It's a short book, but well worth the read. I know a lot of people have only heard that it's the "racy" one that talks about body parts and sex. As a matter of fact, it sort of does. But if you can get past that and look deeper, you'll uncover the greatest love story of all time. I guess I relate to the girl who meets this guy and doesn't think she's good enough for him. He continues to woo her until she hesitantly begins a relationship with him. The story continues as she grows from being only interested in what she wants, to willingly being with him at any cost. Sound familiar? Turns out, this guy was a king. He wasn't just any king, mind you, but the richest and wisest one in all the land. (I know, the stuff every girl's dreams are made of, right?) He even sends a horse-drawn carriage with strong soldiers to keep her safe as they whisk her off to the wedding. Richard Gere's ending limo scene in the movie, Pretty Woman, has nothing on this guy! The story comes to an end with them in a garden where he asks her to go away with him to a place where they can be together always and live happily ever after. (Cue sappy music and heaving sighs.)

The most common fairytales we remember from our childhood days followed a similar storyline and always ended with a prince charming sweeping the young maiden off to an elusive place called "Happily-Ever-After". This particular story, however, happens to be true. Not only was it true back when it was first written, it's true today. I know your immediate thought is, "How is that even possible?". Since you asked, I'm happy to tell you that this story can be an illustration of what it's like to be in a relationship with King Jesus. He's got more going for Him than any king that we can read about in children's books. That's why He's commonly referred to as the King of kings. Just like the king in our story, His greatest desire is to spend forever with the love of His life…YOU! The real turning point for me was when I finally accepted the idea that He even wanted someone like me. He patiently waits for us to fall in love with Him, and then promises that He will take care of everything if we let Him.

Can I just tell you that Jesus is the best wedding planner ever? He understands all you want and need even down to the little things. What a relief to sit back and not have to carry the worry of details and what-ifs! He will always give step-by-step instructions that, if followed, will result in the unfolding of miraculous and magnificent developments on the way to the wedding. According to the Song of Solomon, a carriage comes for the bride. That means that we get a carriage, too! The materials and colors that are used in the construction of this grand coach are descriptively listed in the account. These types of things are important in the Bible. They are not just there to conjure up an image in our imagination, but they are symbolic of deeper things. By this time, I was so excited about the prospect of my ride, I looked up the meaning of every single one.

The carriage was mainly constructed of wood from Lebanon. The cedar trees that grew in that country were very highly sought after. They grew tall and strong. The importance of this tree is evident even now as it has become the emblem on the center of the country's national flag. During the time of the writing of the Old Testament, the reason everyone wanted to build with them was that this wood was of very high quality. It had a wonderful aroma and resisted decay and insects, which made it virtually indestructible. I think this carriage represents the Word of God. It is pliable enough to fit any situation in our lives, yet strong enough to carry us through every storm and circumstance. By the way, the cedars are evergreens, which means they are always covered with green.

That brings us to the topic of the colors of the carriage and their biblical symbolism. With the exception of one place in Leviticus, green is associated with life and growth. Three other colors are specifically mentioned here. There were silver posts and supports of gold. Silver indicates redemption, while gold always stands for divinity. That's an amazing description of our relationship with our King. God loves us so much that He redeems our messes by allowing His Son, Jesus, to give His life in exchange for ours. What an unbelievably unbalanced exchange! Next on the list is a seat of purple. Purple represents royalty. This means that not only do we get the opportunity to have a whole different life, but we get to sit on a throne! And we don't even have to wait until after the ceremony.

There is a smell coming from the carriage of perfumes and fragrant powders. On top of everything else, He provides the makeup which is applied in the carriage. It will be applied for us (which is a good thing considering what disasters have happened when we've attempted to put on our own makeup in a moving vehicle) and will make us more beautiful than we've ever been before. It can make a girl all giddy inside. I imagine the fragrant aromas will just emanate from us so that everyone will smell us as we drive along on our way to the wedding. All of this work can sometimes be tedious and must never be rushed. That's okay, though, because it just might be a very long ride. In fact, it could last a lifetime.

"Let us be glad and rejoice, and let us give honor to him. For the time has come for the wedding feast of the Lamb, and his bride has prepared herself." Revelation 19:7 (NLT)

CHAPTER 11

STAYING BUSY WHILE WE WAIT

I wish I knew the date that Jesus was coming for His bride. So does everybody else that knows about it. Some people are so obsessed with knowing the exact day and hour that they have spent their whole lives trying to figure it out. I can't bring myself to occupy much time on the subject. Frankly, anything that has to do with that much calculation hurts my brain. Math never came easily to me - especially word problems. With all of the searching for hints in the Bible and what we know is going on around us, to then come up with a date and time reminds me too much of the equations I dreaded having to come up with! It's enough for me to know with the confidence that comes only from knowing Him so well that He is true to His word. He will come. In the meantime, we shouldn't just be twiddling our thumbs and watching the world pass by through the windows of the carriage as we ride along on our way to the ceremony.

There are just times when a girl's got to pull out her cell phone and start talking or texting. That's a great way to pass the time! And with the addition of social media, minutes can quickly turn into hours. Before you know it, the whole day is shot. Now please don't start sending all the hate posts to my accounts. Obviously, this technology has become so popular because it can be very useful. I wouldn't have them if I didn't believe that. Nothing can gladden our hearts like logging on and seeing pictures of our grandchildren or families posted from far away. Okay, maybe they just live a few minutes away, but you experience the same reaction. Friends we haven't been in contact with for years suddenly seem like an integral part of our lives. There are memories shared as well as news of sickness, pain, and tragedy. Special occasions of every kind come with pictures and great details of the events and everyone who follows knows about it- even those around the globe we have never met!

Like any other bride, I want everyone in the world to know about my upcoming wedding. I am positive that even if they roll their eyes and shake their heads, unfriend me on Facebook, or turn and run for the hills, this will be the greatest event that ever took place. One thing I know for sure is that my behavior can't be like the bridezillas we've all encountered if I want to have any chance of them even listening, let alone actually paying attention. How we act always precedes what we say in the minds of the people watching us. Remember that old saying your mother taught you as a child, "Actions speak louder than words"? There is a reason those old clichés have stayed around so long, handed down from one generation to the next. It's because they were all spoken by people who discovered their truths while dealing with the circumstances in their own lives that taught them that particular lesson.

Jesus gave a ton of examples about how we should conduct ourselves in every situation imaginable in the Bible. It's not a list of do's and don'ts, but another part of dressing for the wedding that He'll gladly help us with so that everyone will

61

want to know all about our love affair. He said one last thing before He left to build for us the biggest and best house we've ever lived in. Tell everybody. Go around the world and let everyone know about the greatest love story that's ever happened. He wants them all to be His bride. The majority of us don't have the kind of resources it would take to fund that kind of trip. If you love to travel like I do, I'm sure you wish you did. But remember those cell phones we talked about? In addition, we have computers, tablets, and the ever reliable pen and paper. Last time I looked, our neighborhood grocery stores or gas stations were part of the world. We've all struck up conversations while standing in line at the store or pumping gas. We have to get busy and tell someone! Let's start in our own homes.

Our children are our most precious possessions. We always want what's best for them. The very best thing we can do for them is to teach them about Jesus. We can't just tell them about Him. We need to show them how wonderful He is and model before them your own relationship with Him. Let them catch you talking to Him when they come bursting into the room and no one else is around. Let them know how important your Bible is to you and that it is the very source of everything good in your life. Let them see you pouring over its pages. Let them know that it contains the very words of God and they are all true. For those that are married, let that relationship be a vivid picture of the selfless, forever relationship that we read about between its covers. Tell your little "fair maidens" that they have value and worth. That they are beautiful in every way, not just on the outside. Build their confidence and self-esteem by speaking kind words and reminding them that they were created for a very special purpose that was planned for them long before they were born. Then do everything you can to help them discover what that purpose is. Do the same things for those "prince charmings" as you teach them that they will one day be given the honor and responsibility of representing Jesus to their own family. More than anything else we can do for them, we need to spend time talking to Jesus about these kids. Ask for His help when it comes to showing them how to allow the Bridegroom to prepare them for the wedding and teaching them what to do while they wait. Show them that the key to this whole thing is getting to know Him so well that all they want to do is what He says and the only place they want to be is where He is.

In this life, we all make decisions. We all organize priorities because of our hectic schedules and all that we're expected to accomplish. The demands of life can scream louder than the voice of our Beloved if we let it. When I reflect on where I was and where I find myself today, even those that have known me most of my life are amazed at the transformation. Believe me when I tell you, I'm not yet where He wants me to be. I'm just a girl on her way to join her Prince Charming, allowing Him to continue to dress her while the carriage moves her through the real world as she waits. After all, I want to be the prettiest one at the wedding!

"Watch, therefore [give strict attention and be cautious and active], for you know neither the day nor the hour when the Son of Man will come." Matthew 25:13 (AMP)

CHAPTER 12

YOUR INVITATION HAS ARRIVED

Prince Charming always comes on a shiny white horse to get his true love and sweep her away to live happily ever after. Unlike all the other stories you've read, the one described here is not fiction. This one is for real. Jesus will, indeed, return on a white horse! He wants for you to be His Bride- believers from around the world, both male and female. That's right! For you guys that were brave enough to pick up and read my story, I know that it must be hard for you to wrap your brain around the possibility of you being anybody's bride. I want you to realize that broken lives and longing hearts have no gender. You, too, can experience the love of an intimate relationship with the One who loved you first and loves you best.

If there's even a small tugging on your heart that's betraying your disappointments, fears, wounds or pain, that's your invitation. Now's your chance to accept it. If your RSVP is "yes", just say these words out loud:

"Jesus, thank You for loving me so much that you gave your very own life so that I can spend mine with You. I've made a mess of things and I don't know how to navigate this road in this real world. Please come into my life and help me. I give it to You and allow You to heal my heart, and get me dressed, transformed, and ready for the time when I get to see You face-to-face."

It's that simple. Nothing complicated or hard to understand. If you said those words and really meant them, congratulations! Put on your seatbelt, strap yourself into the carriage, and never get out —no matter what. You're about to experience the most amazing trip of your life!

"The Spirit and the bride say, 'Come.'. Let anyone who hears this say, 'Come.' Let anyone who is thirsty come. Let anyone

who desires drink freely from the water of life." Revelation 22:17 (NLT)

If you just made this decision, please contact me at establishingword.com and let me know so that I can celebrate with you. Also, I encourage you to find a church in your area* and make some friends there. We all need some support and encouragement on our journey. Lastly, don't forget to tell someone!

*Suggested link: www.churchfinder.com.Ag.org

ABOUT THE AUTHOR

SALLY SMALE is a dynamic speaker who has a heart to teach and train others to extravagantly fulfill God's purposes in their lives and for the kingdom of God. She helps to identify and bring forth gifts and callings in people that they haven't recognized or have left dormant for years. Her use of humor and real transparency has led to healing and deliverance for many. A credentialed minister, Sally and her husband, Mark, co-pastor a church in southern Arizona. Married for more than four decades, they have 3 adult sons and 3 daughters-in-love who have blessed them with 9 amazing grandchildren. They are all keeping busy while they are "Waiting for Prince Charming in the Real World".